SNOWBOARDING

Rennay Craats

Weigl Publishers Inc.

Published by Weigl Publishers Inc.
123 South Broad Street, Box 227
Mankato, MN 56002
USA
Copyright © 2002 Weigl Publishers Inc.
Web site: www.weigl.com

Library of Congress Cataloging-in-Publication
Data available upon request from the publisher.
Fax: (507) 388-2746 for the attention of the
Publishing Records Department.
ISBN: 1-930954-37-9

Printed in the United States of America
1 2 3 4 5 6 7 8 9 05 04 03 02 01

Managing Editor
Kara Turner
Layout and Design
Warren Clark
Terry Paulhus
Susan Kenyon
Copy Editor
Jennifer Nault

Photograph credits
Cover: Corbis Images; Corbis Images: page 6, 7,
8L, 10R, 14L, 16T, 18L, 19L, 21, 23R; Empics
Sports Photography Ltd: page 9B, 11, 13R, 15, 17;
Eyewire: page 1, 8R, 12, 20R, 20L, 22; Kurt Hoy:
page 3, 9T, 10L, 14R, 16B, 19R; PhotoDisc Ltd:
page 4, 5B, 13L, 23L.

Contents

What is Snowboarding?

Snowboarding began in the mid-1960s. One of the first snowboards was invented by Sherman Poppen. It looked like a water ski with a rope on the front and was called a "Snurfer." Snowboarders held on to the rope and stood on the board like a surfboard. It was difficult to stay on and steer the board. In 1963, a teenager named Tom Sims

became frustrated that he could not skateboard in winter. He created a skateboard for snow in his wood-shop class. He later improved and redesigned his board. Soon, more people were trying snowboarding. Over the years, snowboarding has become more popular, and ski hills are now filled with snowboarders of all ages and abilities.

Snowboarding is sometimes described as "surfing on snow."

4

Snowboarding is a combination of several sports. It has many of the same movements as surfing, but like skiing it is done on a snow hill. Snowboarders also perform skateboarding tricks. Snowboarders shift their weight from side to side as they glide over the snow. Unlike skiers, snowboarders do not use poles, and they stop by digging the board into the side of the hill. As snowboarders improve their skills, they can try more challenging ski runs or learn tricks on a ramp of snow called a **halfpipe**.

Halfpipes provide a location for snowboarders to practice tricks. These moves require balance and strength.

CHECK IT OUT

For trick tips and photographs, surf over to
www.snowblown.com

5

Getting Ready to Board

Snowboarders need to wrap up warm and protect themselves from the wind, snow, and sun when stepping onto the slopes. They also have to decide what kind of snowboard they are going to use. Stiff boards are faster and are designed for **carving** at high speeds. Boards with some flexibility are better for beginner snowboarders.

Snowboarders wear goggles or sunglasses while on the slopes. Eyewear should be tinted to protect against the sun and glare from the snow.

Wearing a helmet is always a good idea while snowboarding. It prevents head injuries during a fall.

Just because it is cold does not mean the sun's rays are not harmful. Snowboarders should wear sunscreen to avoid burning.

Waterproof pants are popular snowboarding clothes. Some boarders like to wear long underwear to stay warm.

The snowboard is the most important piece of equipment. The length of a snowboard depends on the user's height and weight. A snowboard should stand between the boarder's chin and nose when it is upright. The front and back edges of the board are turned up. This prevents the board from getting stuck in the snow when snowboarders perform tricks. The side cut allows snowboarders to keep their boards touching the snow when they turn. If there is a lot of side cut, the turns can be difficult for beginners to control.

Bindings are plastic fastenings that hold snowboarders' feet on to the board. Bindings have a foot strap. Riders keep this strap around an ankle so their snowboard will not slide away from them if they fall.

Most snowboarders wear a waterproof jacket when it is cold or snowing. If it is warm, some boarders wear a sweater over a long-sleeved shirt.

Gloves protect against cold weather and snow that sprays up as snowboarders glide down the slope.

The Slopes

Snowboarding can be done just about anywhere downhill skiing is enjoyed. As is the case with skiers, snowboarders need to know how difficult each slope is. Runs are classified according to difficulty. Easy runs are often marked with a green circle. Intermediate runs are often labeled with a blue square. Difficult and very difficult runs are marked with one or two black diamonds. If snowboarders choose to board elsewhere, they need to make sure the slopes are not at risk of **avalanches**.

Some people take snowboarding to the extreme and board in steep, rocky, or remote areas. These riders combine mountain awareness with their snowboarding skills.

Extreme snowboarders carry avalanche gear, spare clothing, and other safety equipment.

8

Snowboarders who simply want to board down the slopes stick to regular runs. Those who are performing tricks do not. Snowboarding tricks can be dangerous. To make sure all skiers and snowboarders are safe, many snowboarding tricks can only be done in **designated** snowboarding areas. Parks are also built with jumps and other snow obstacles. These areas have halfpipes for boarders to practice their tricks.

Once riders can control their boards, they learn how to perform tricks in a halfpipe.

Halfpipes are carved out of snow using machines called pipe dragons. These large machines create the correct slope on the snow ramp.

CHECK IT OUT

For information on resorts, head to

www.skitelevision.com

9

Rules of Competition

There are two main types of snowboarding competitions. Alpine is a racing event that requires boarders to maneuver around flags. **Freestyle** events feature tricks performed on a halfpipe. There are variations or combinations of these events. For example, boardercross is a combination of both styles. Slopestyle competitions are similar to halfpipe events but are done in snowboard parks.

Some snowboarders like to board at top speed, while others prefer tricks. The sport offers something for everyone.

Each event has its own rules. In the alpine, or slalom, event, boarders are **disqualified** if they miss a flag. They are also disqualified if they enter the course while judges are inspecting it. Otherwise, judges could get hurt as boarders travel at up to 50 miles per hour. The competitor who finishes the course with the fastest time wins the competition.

As in alpine competitions, boardercross competitors cannot miss flags or leave the competition area. If they do, they will be disqualified.

10

Freestyle competitions have rules, too. For safety reasons, only a limited number of people are allowed to warm up on a halfpipe at one time. If competitors enter the halfpipe outside their set time, they are disqualified. Also, if competitors fall during their first jump on the halfpipe, they have only 2 minutes to try the jump again.

Judges are on hand to make sure rules are followed. They also rate tricks in freestyle competitions. They look for tricks that are difficult but are made to look easy. They also rate the height a boarder achieves off a jump and how well he or she lands. Original tricks earn more points. During competitions, judges look for both skill and creativity. Snowboarders are always trying to invent new jumps, or **airs**, to impress the judges, spectators, and other competitors.

Music is often played at unofficial contests, such as "Big Air" competitions. Riders can listen to the latest sounds while jumping or "getting air."

CHECK IT OUT

Check out the U.S. Snowboard Association Web site at

www.usasa.org

11

Learning the Moves

To begin with, snowboarders need to learn to fall. This is called biffing. Even professional boarders fall while learning and performing new tricks. Boarders need to avoid using their hands when they fall. Instead, they should bend at the knees and waist and fall on their elbows and knees. This way, they are less likely to get hurt.

Another important skill is stopping. The side-slip helps boarders to slow down or stop. Snowboarders direct their boards so they are facing across the hill rather than down. Then they tilt the board up into the edge of the hill. This stops the board from moving. To start sliding again, they slowly bring the board down flat on the snow.

Snowboarders shift their weight from heels to toes, as well as from one end of the board to the other.

CHECK IT OUT

To learn more techniques and tricks, head to

www.boardpass.com/ snowboardsite.html

12

Another necessary snowboarding skill is turning. To turn, snowboarders shift their weight from one side of the board to the other. Putting weight on the front foot makes the board head downhill. During toe turns, boarders lean the board to the edge closest to their toes. To perform a heel turn, boarders place their weight over the edge of the board closest to their heels. Combining these two turns allows snowboarders to zigzag down the hill.

Snowboarding offers many tricks. An ollie is the most basic one and enables boarders to jump in the air without using ramps. Boarders start an ollie with their knees slightly bent and arms out for balance. Then they shift their weight to their back foot. By springing forward and upward off the back of the snowboard, boarders lift themselves off the ground. They land **nose** first to finish the trick.

Snowboarding turns should be made in one smooth motion. Boarders keep their weight forward.

An ollie can be done off ramps to get even greater height. It can be combined with other moves for more complicated tricks.

13

Tricks of the Sport

Airs are jumps done while on a snowboard. Boarders ride over mounds of snow of different sizes. The basic ollie and other tricks can be made more exciting by using different hand grabs. Boarders can reach down with one hand to grab the board in different places while soaring through the air. Reaching between their feet to the heel-side of the board with their front hand is called a chicken salad. Reaching their back hand to the toe side of the board is called an indie. These and other grabs help create different tricks.

Watching experienced snowboarders is a great way to learn new moves.

Boarders need to get plenty of height when attempting tricks.

14

Once the basic tricks are mastered, snowboarders can add flips and more complicated moves. A backscratcher is an exciting trick. To perform it, boarders bend their knees at the height of their jump and grab the board. The snowboard rests against their back. Boarders need to make sure they jump high enough to finish this trick. If they are too low, they will not be able to straighten their legs in time for the landing.

Mid-air flips and turns are popular with snowboarders. Boarders use halfpipes to perform moves such as the frontside air, nuclear air, eggplant, McTwist, and Phillips 66. Most of these flips and turns require a great deal of skill and practice. Other moves are similar to skateboarding tricks, such as sliding along rails, or performing moves on flat ground.

Boarders use different holds as they perform everything from a handstand on a halfpipe rim to a complete spin off a jump.

Boarding for Gold

Many adventurous athletes look to snowboarding for a challenge. Most ski resorts and hills offer snowboarding lessons. Once beginners learn to control their boards, the sky is the limit. Practicing on easy runs helps snowboarders gain confidence and skill. They slowly add harder tricks and tackle tougher runs. Snowboarding often starts out as a hobby, but it can turn into a competitive sport.

Powder is fresh snow that is light and deep. Snowboarders love to make new tracks through the powder.

A competitor at the X Games excites onlookers with a backside method.

There are many competitions approved by organizations such as the International Snowboard Federation (ISF) and the International Ski Federation (FIS). Events attract a great deal of attention worldwide. The X Games, which feature extreme sports such as snowboarding, skateboarding, BMX riding, and inline skating, host popular tournaments. Winners receive prize money and attract sponsors to help finance them. The World Cup for snowboarding is another **prestigious** event. It is the highest level of **amateur** competition. Some athletes want to remain amateurs so they can compete at the Olympic Games. The Olympics included snowboarding for the first time in 1998. This was exciting for snowboarders because it showed that the sport had been accepted.

The first competitive snowboarding event was held in Leadville, Colorado, in 1981. Snowboarders can now compete in many different events.

CHECK IT OUT

To find out about snowboarding at the 2002 Winter Olympic Games, visit

www.saltlake2002.com

17

Superstars of the Sport

Snowboarding heroes make the sport more exciting to watch.

CARA-BETH BURNSIDE

DATE OF BIRTH:
July 23, 1968
HOMETOWN:
Orange, California

Career Facts:

- Cara-Beth began snowboarding in 1990.
- Cara-Beth was one of eight women chosen for the U.S. Olympic snowboarding team. She competed in the halfpipe competition in Nagano, Japan, in 1998.
- In 1998, Cara-Beth won a gold medal in halfpipe snowboarding at the X Games.
- Cara-Beth is one of the best female skateboarders as well. She has become a spokesperson for women in sports.
- Several companies sponsor Cara-Beth.

ANDY HETZEL

DATE OF BIRTH:
July 6, 1969
HOMETOWN:
Tahoe City, California

Career Facts:

- Andy has won boardercross and slopestyle competitions around the world.
- Since 1997, Andy has finished in the top ten at X Games competitions seven times.
- Andy's signature move is a front flip with a 360-degree twist.
- Andy uses his knowledge and enthusiasm for the sport to design his own boards.
- Andy has appeared in many snowboarding videos.

CRAIG KELLY

BIRTH DATE:
1967
HOMETOWN:
Mount Vernon,
Washington

Career Facts:

- Craig entered his first competition in 1984 and won the World Slalom Championship only two years later.
- Craig won seven World Championship titles in his snowboarding career.
- From 1988 to 1998, Craig ran a snowboarding camp. He also participated in a snowboarding program for underprivileged children called Chill.
- Craig was a star in all different areas of snowboarding. He won the National Championship for freestyle, **moguls**, and slalom three times.
- In 1991, Craig retired from competition.

ROSS POWERS

BIRTH DATE:
February 10, 1979
HOMETOWN:
South Londonderry,
Vermont

Career Facts:

- Ross has been competing since he was in the fourth grade.
- Ross is a member of the U.S. snowboard team. He won a bronze medal in the first men's halfpipe competition at the 1998 Olympics.
- In 1998, Ross finished first in the halfpipe and slopestyle events at the X Games.
- Ross won gold medals in the halfpipe at the Gravity Games and the Goodwill Games in 2000.
- In 2000, Ross was the overall ISF World Halfpipe Champion and the USSA National Champion. He also won all three Triple Crown halfpipe events.
- A number of companies sponsor Ross.

CHECK IT OUT

Find out more about the U.S. snowboarding team at
www.usskiteam.com/snowboard/snowboard.htm

19

Getting in Shape

Snowboarding is a very physical sport. Athletes need to be fit and strong to perform their tricks and enjoy the sport. Eating a balanced diet is important. Fruit and vegetables, breads and cereals, and milk and milk products help keep athletes healthy. Drinking plenty of water is also very important before, during, and after exercising. Athletes need to replace the water they lose through sweating, even when the weather is cold.

Snowboarding is tough on leg muscles. Many snowboarders go to the gym in between trips to the slopes.

Fruit and vegetables provide essential vitamins and minerals, as well as dietary fiber.

No snowboarder just steps onto a snowboard and starts doing tricks. They warm up first and do some stretching. Stretching before starting any vigorous exercise helps prevent injuries. Snowboarding uses many muscle groups, so athletes need to make sure they stretch their leg, arm, and back muscles before stepping onto the slopes. Even after stretching, they do not start doing difficult tricks right away. They snowboard down the hill without performing any tricks to get their bodies warmed up. Then they can begin performing tricks.

Snowboarding is an energetic sport. Riders need to warm up thoroughly before heading onto the slopes.

CHECK IT OUT

To learn more about healthy eating, head to
www.healthyeating.org/kids

21

Brain Teasers

How much do you know about snowboarding? See if you can answers these questions!

Q What is a spine?

A A spine is a rim of snow or a rail on which snowboarders perform tricks.

Q Why was snowboarding banned on ski hills in the sport's early years?

A Many people thought snowboarders were wild and dangerous. After a while, people realized that snowboarding was no more dangerous than skiing.

Q What is "shredding"?

A Shredding is riding fast and stylishly. Snowboarders "shred" the mountain on their snowboards.

Q Is it possible to snowboard without snow?

A Yes. Some people snowboard on sand.

Q How do snowboarders move on level ground without poles?

A Snowboarders only strap their front foot into the bindings when on flat ground or the chairlift. That way they can use their back foot to move them forward.

Q What is "goofy foot"?

A Riding on a snowboard with the right foot in the forward position. In other words, the right foot is closest to the nose, furthest from the tail.

23

Glossary

airs: tricks performed off the ground

amateur: someone who does something as a hobby and not as a profession

avalanches: large amounts of snow or ice that fall or slide down a mountainside

carving: turning

designated: marked for a particular purpose

disqualified: not allowed to compete in a contest after breaking the rules

freestyle: style of snowboarding in which the rider uses halfpipes to perform tricks

halfpipe: a U-shaped chute built in the snow

moguls: large bumps of snow on a slope that are a challenge to ride

nose: front tip of the snowboard

prestigious: having a good reputation due to past success

Index

airs 11, 13, 14, 15
alpine 10
avalanche 8
backscratcher 15
biffing 12
binding 7, 23
boardercross 10, 18
Burnside, Cara-Beth 18

diet 20
freestyle 10, 11, 19
halfpipe 5, 9, 10, 11, 15, 18, 19
Hetzel, Andy 18
Kelly, Craig 19
ollie 13, 14
Olympic Games 17, 18, 19

parks 9, 10
Poppen, Sherman 4
Powers, Ross 19
Sims, Tom 4
skateboard 4, 5, 17, 18
surfing 4, 5
X Games 16, 17, 18, 19

Web Sites

www.snowblown.com
www.skitelevision.com
www.usasa.org

www.boardpass.com/snowboardsite.html
www.saltlake2002.com
www.healthyeating.org/kids

www.usskiteam.com/snowboard/snowboard.htm